Insects
and
Spiders

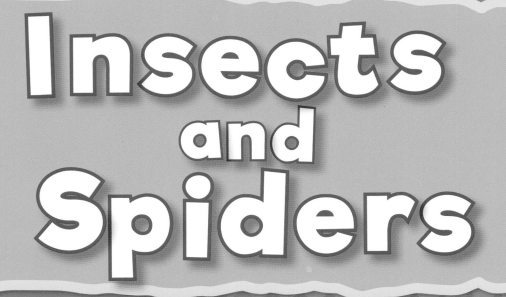

DAWN TITMUS

Published in 2019 by The Rosen
Publishing Group, Inc.
29 East 21st Street, New York, NY 10010

Cataloging-in-Publication Data

Names: Titmus, Dawn.
Title: Insects and spiders / Dawn Titmus.
Description: New York : PowerKids Press, 2019. | Series: Cool pets for kids | Includes glossary and index.
Identifiers: LCCN ISBN 9781538338025 (pbk.) | ISBN 9781538338018 (library bound) |
ISBN 9781538338032 (6 pack)
Subjects: LCSH: Insects as pets--Juvenile literature. | Spiders as pets--Juvenile literature.
Classification: LCC SF459.I5 T58 2019 | DDC 638'.5--dc23

Text and editor: Dawn Titmus
Editorial Director: Lindsey Lowe
Children's Publisher: Anne O'Daly
Design Manager: Keith Davis
Picture Manager: Sophie Mortimer

Photo acknowledgements:
t=top, c=center, b=bottom, l=left, r=right
Alamy: blickwinkel 18; Ardea: Pascal Goetgheluck 9b; Dreamstime: Ghostprophet 22, Photographerlondon
6b; iStock: BanyanRanchStudios 17b, ConstantinosZ 9t, Thomas Demarczky 11b, eyfoto 21t, JanMiko 29c,
mtreasure 25b, nycshooter 29t, SHAWSHANK61 19t, skydie 15t, Sziban 15b, wanderluster 12; Photoshot:
Picture Alliance/C. Steimer 6t, 7; Shutterstock: Aedka Studio 5b, Pathara Buranadilok 13t, Andrew Burgress
13b, Linn Currie 23t, evantravels 29b, Oleksandr Hrinchenko 21b, Vitalii Hulai 1l, Hurst Photo 5t, Eric Isselee
4b, JDCarballo 24, Cathy Keifer 10-11, Mirek Kijewski 26, D. Kucharski/K. Kucharska 8, 16, Oleksandr
Lytvynenko 3, Anukool Manoton 1r, Narin Nonthamland 27b, NowhereLand Photography 14b, Olgysha 4-5,
PHOTOCREO/Michal Bednarek 1c, PK Phuket Studio 11t, Zaidi Razak 19b, skydie 23b, Audrey Snider-Bell 27t,
Dejan Stanisavljevic 25t, Maxal Tamor 10, Marek Velechovsky 17t, Connie Wade 20, yurakrasil 4t.

Manufactured in the United States of America

CPSIA Compliance Information: Batch #CSPK18: For Further Information contact Rosen Publishing, New York,
New York at 1-800-237-9932.

Contents

Which Insect or Spider? 4

What You Will Need 6

Housing Your Pet 8

Feeding Time 10

Staying Healthy 12

In the Wild 14

Vietnamese Walking Stick 16

Orchid Mantis 18

Madagascar Hissing
    Cockroach 20

Honduran Curly
    Hair Tarantula 22

Chilean Rose Tarantula 24

Mexican Redknee Tarantula .. 26

Make It!: Bug Hotel 28

Did You Know? 29

Glossary 30

Further Resources 31

Index 32

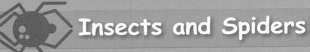
Which Insect or Spider?

Insects and spiders are fascinating pets. They are easy to look after and do not need much space. However, they do need some care and attention.

Best for Beginners

It is best to start with an insect or spider that is not too delicate or dangerous. Hissing cockroaches are robust and don't bite or sting. Stick bugs and leaf insects are more delicate, but they are easy to care for. Some tarantulas are good for beginners, such as the Mexican redknee. Usually, these spiders are quite docile. Make sure no one in your family is afraid of spiders before you get one as a pet!

Local Laws

Be sure to check your local laws. In some states, it's illegal to keep certain pet spiders or insects. For example, Indian walking sticks are a plant pest in the US.

Learn the Basics

Find out what your pet needs to eat and how it should be housed before you bring it home. Some insects can live happily in a jar. Spiders that come from warm regions need to have their home at a certain temperature.

The Right Insect or Spider for You?

☑ Have you found out what food and housing your pet insect or spider needs?

☑ Can you look after a spider for many years? Some tarantulas can live for 25 years or more.

☑ Will you have time to care for your pet?

☑ Is everyone in your family happy for you to keep a pet insect or spider?

☑ Is it permitted to keep the insect or spider in your state?

Read On ...

Insects and spiders are cool pets and are a lot of fun, but it is important to choose the right one. This book will help you to choose and care for your pet. Learn about six popular types of insects and spiders and try your hand at making a bug hotel. You will also find some fascinating facts about your new insect and spider friends!

What You Will Need

One of the most important things you will need is your pet's home. You may have to heat it to a certain temperature and keep the humidity high.

Housing Your Pet

Stick bugs need an enclosure that is three times as long as their body. Leaf insects can live in either a plastic or a glass tank, or even a large candy jar. Cockroaches are good climbers. They will need a cage with a tight lid. Tarantulas need a glass or plastic tank of at least 2.5 gallons (9.5 liters).

Special Diets

Leaf and stick insects eat bramble (blackberry), oak, hawthorn, or rose leaves. You will need to find a regular supply of these leaves in your yard or neighborhood.

Water Sprayer

Most insects and some spiders need a high level of humidity in their enclosure. Use a humidity gauge to check the level. Lightly spray inside the enclosure with a water sprayer to keep it humid.

Keeping It Warm

Most cockroaches and tarantulas come from warm regions. They need their housing to be kept at 77°F (25°C) or more. Check the room temperature in your home with a thermometer. If it's too cold, you can heat the enclosure by placing it near a light bulb or using heat mats. Heat mats go under part of the enclosure and plug into a power source.

What You Need

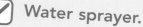 Tank or other container for housing.

✓ The right food for your pet.

✓ Water sprayer.

✓ Humidity gauge and thermometer.

✓ Heat mat for some pets.

 Shallow water container.

 Small-animal keeper (for live food).

Live Food

Mantids and tarantulas need to eat live foods, such as crickets and mealworms. If you keep the live food at home, you will need a secure enclosure for it. You will also need to feed it well and give it water.

Housing Your Pet

Enclosures for pet insects and spiders range from small plastic containers to large glass tanks. Clean out the enclosure every four to six months.

Cockroaches

A 10-gallon (38-liter) fish tank will house up to 30 large adult roaches. Fit a secure mesh lid—cockroaches are good climbers. Line the bottom of the tank with wood shavings or coconut fiber. Roaches like hiding places, such as pieces of bark, paper egg cartons, or cardboard tubes.

Stick and Leaf Insects

A 10-gallon (38-liter) glass fish tank or terrarium makes a good home for these insects. Stick bugs hang down from plants to shed their skins (molt). They need the enclosure to be three times as high as the insect. Put some twigs and leaves inside the tank. Cover the bottom with a substrate, such as moss or peat. Cover the top with mesh or netting.

Mantids

It is usually best to keep a pet mantid on its own. Two or more in an enclosure will fight. Your mantid needs space and a branch to hang from when it sheds its skin. The top of the branch needs to be at least three times the length of the mantid. Find out the right humidity level and temperature for your mantid. Most mantids need a warm container at 70 to 90°F (21 to 32°C).

Spiders

Your spider needs a home that is about three times as long as its leg span and twice as wide. You can use a glass fish tank with a tightly fitting lid. You could also use a plastic box with a snap-on lid. Make holes in the lid to let air in. If you have a tree-dwelling spider, it will need a tall enclosure with branches inside. Line the bottom of the tank with bedding. Find out what type of material is best for your spider and what the temperature and humidity in the tank should be.

Feeding Time

Different types of insects and spiders need different types of food. Find out what food is best to give your pet and how often you need to feed it.

Bramble leaves

Stick and Leaf Insects

Stick and leaf insects like to feed on bramble (blackberry) leaves. Some also like oak, hawthorn, and raspberry leaves. Be sure to collect leaves that have not been sprayed with insecticide. Collect leaves away from busy roads, as the leaves may be poisoned by traffic fumes. Always wash the leaves before you give them to your pet.

Mantids

Mantids eat live food. Young or small mantids eat small insects such as fruit flies and aphids. Adult mantids eat larger food such as house flies, moths, and crickets. You can buy live food for mantids, called feeder insects, at the pet store. Put a shallow dish of water inside the tank. Put a sponge or some pebbles in the dish so your mantid does not drown in the water.

Cockroaches

Cockroaches eat more or less anything! Feed them a mixture of dried food, such as oats or dog food, and fresh fruit and vegetables. Roaches like apples, bananas, and carrots. Give your pets water in a shallow dish. Put a sponge or some pebbles in the dish so your roaches do not drown.

Spiders

Spiders are meat-eaters. Most of them eat insects. Tarantulas eat crickets, and some eat lizards and small mice. Most tarantulas need only one or two crickets once a week. You could also feed a tarantula mealworms, beetles, and cockroaches. Feed your spider food that is no bigger than its abdomen. Put a shallow dish of water in the tank with a sponge or pebbles inside to prevent your pet from drowning.

Staying Healthy

Providing your pet with a spacious home, fresh water, and the right kind of food will help keep it healthy. Check your insect or spider every day for signs of sickness.

Delicate Sticks

Take great care when handling stick insects. Their long, thin legs and body are fragile. Rough handling could cause a stick insect to lose a leg. Overcrowding can also lead to limb loss. Young stick insects can regrow a lost limb when they molt. Adults no longer molt, so usually they are not able to regrow a leg.

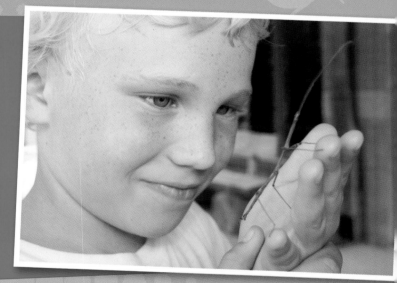

Molting Mantids

Most mantids need their tank to be humid. If it is too dry when they molt, they could struggle to shed the layer of skin and may lose a leg. A young mantid can regrow a leg at the next molt. Adults no longer molt, so they are not able to regrow a leg.

Hairy Tarantulas

Make sure your pet has hiding spaces in the tank. Spiders can become stressed if they have nowhere to hide. Ground-dwelling tarantulas should not have objects to climb in the tank. They can hurt themselves if they fall. Tarantulas are especially fragile when they are molting.

Signs That Your Tarantula Is Going to Molt

- ✓ It is lying on its back.
- ✓ It stops eating.
- ✓ It becomes slow and sluggish.
- ✓ It develops a bald spot on its abdomen.
- ✓ It turns a dull color.

Molting is a stressful time for your pet. Do not feed it when it's molting and for five days afterward.

Robust Roaches

Cockroaches are hardy creatures. They can be easily handled, although their antennae can be fragile. Make sure that your pet roaches have enough food. They may nibble their tank mates' wings or antennae if they are not fed regularly. Also make sure that the humidity level is right for your roaches, particularly when they are molting.

In the Wild

Insects live all over the world. There is a tiny fly that can even survive the icy cold of Antarctica and a cockroach that lives in the Arctic. Spiders live in most areas, apart from polar regions.

Stick and Leaf Insects

Stick bugs live all over the world, particularly in tropical regions. They live and feed on the leaves of plants. Leaf insects live in Southeast Asia. Stick and leaf insects look like the plants on which they live. In 2016, a Chinese museum bred a stick bug that grew to 25 inches (64 cm) long.

Tropical Tarantulas

Tarantulas are known as bird-eating spiders, but few of them actually eat birds. Most tarantulas live in forests in tropical areas of the world, although some have adapted to live in deserts. The largest is the Goliath tarantula of northern South America. It has a leg span of more than 10 inches (25 cm).

Roaches Everywhere

Cockroaches live in most places, including deserts, grasslands, and forests. Some burrow in the ground and live in caves. The American, German, Oriental, and Australian cockroaches have become regular unwelcome guests in people's homes. Most cockroaches are about the size of a thumbnail. One of the largest is the Central American giant cave cockroach. It is 3 to 4 inches (7.5 to 10 cm) long.

Mantids of the World

Mantids live in the warmer regions of the world. They have large eyes, a triangular head, and chewing mouthparts. Their front legs are lined with hooks and spines. They use these to grasp their prey. Most mantids are the same color as the plants around them. Some mantids can change color to match the changing color in plants. Some mantids even resemble flowers, such as the pink-and-white orchid mantis.

Vietnamese Walking Stick

This stick bug is long and thin. It is more active at night and stays almost motionless during the day.

The Vietnamese walking stick looks like a thin green twig.

Where in the World?

As its name suggests, this stick insect comes from Vietnam in Southeast Asia. In the wild, it lives in tropical forests.

16

Breed Profile

The Vietnamese walking stick is most commonly green, but it can also be brown. It has threadlike antennae. Its body is about 6 inches (15 cm) long, and it has a long, oval-shaped head. It rocks back and forth, looking like a twig shaking in the breeze. It lives for about six to seven months.

Looking After Me

The enclosure can be kept at a room temperature of about 68°F (20°C) or warmer. It can be kept cooler at night.

- ☑ Mist the enclosure with a little water every other day.

- ☑ Give your pet a constant supply of fresh bramble leaves. It will also eat oak, hazelnut, rose, or raspberry leaves.

Orchid Mantis

The orchid mantis is a praying mantid. Praying mantids get their name from the position of their front legs when they are resting. They look like they are praying.

The orchid mantis is an eye-catching pink-and-white color.

Where in the World?

In the wild, the orchid mantis lives in the rain forests of Malaysia and Indonesia in Southeast Asia. It feeds on flying insects.

Breed Profile

The orchid mantis looks like a pink-and-white flower. In the wild, its resemblance to a flower attracts insects. Adult females grow to about 2.5 inches (7 cm) long. Males are about 1 inch (2.5 cm) long. The orchid mantis lives for about a year.

Looking After Me

The enclosure needs to be kept at about 82°F (28°C) during the day. At night, the temperature can be allowed to drop to 68°F (20°C).

☑ Spray the tank every day to keep the humidity level at around 60 to 80 percent.

☑ Feed your pet flying insects, such as house flies, bluebottles, or fruit flies, every day. Also give it crickets occasionally.

Madagascar Hissing Cockroach

As its name suggests, the Madagascar hissing cockroach makes hissing sounds! Both males and females hiss when they are disturbed. Males also hiss when they are fighting or looking for a mate.

Where in the World?

This cockroach comes from Madagascar, a large island off the coast of East Africa. It lives on the forest floor in logs and feeds on fruit that has fallen from trees.

The hissing cockroach likes to be handled.

Breed Profile

The Madagascan hissing cockroach is docile and can be handled. It grows to about 1.5 to 3 inches (4 to 8 cm) long. It is dark reddish brown to black. Males have large horns behind the head and hairy antennae. Females have no horns and have smooth antennae. These cockroaches usually live for about two to three years.

Looking After Me

Keep the temperature in the tank above 80°F (26°C) if you want your roaches to grow quickly and breed.

- ☑ Feed your pets dry dog food every day, as well as fruits and vegetables, such as apples and squash.

- ☑ Provide water in a shallow dish with cotton or sponge inside.

Honduran Curly Hair Tarantula

Also known as the wooly tarantula, the Honduran curly hair tarantula is covered in fine golden hairs.

The Honduran curly hair tarantula looks a bit like a cuddly teddy bear!

Where in the World?

The Honduran curly hair tarantula lives in the tropical rain forests of Costa Rica and Honduras, in Central America. In the wild, it lives near water sources such as rivers.

Breed Profile

Some tarantulas flick hairs, called urticating hairs, off their bodies when they feel threatened. The hairs can be irritating to eyes, skin, and throat. The Honduran curly hair has urticating hairs, but it is unlikely to flick them because it is a docile and friendly spider. It is a ground dweller and has a leg span of 5 to 5.5 inches (13 to 14 cm). Females live from 8 to 10 years. Males live for only about four years.

Looking After Me

Keep the temperature in the tank at about 75 to 85°F (24 to 29°C).

✓ The humidity in the tank should be around 75 to 85 percent.

✓ Feed crickets and smaller insects to your pet. Larger pets can be fed a pinky mouse occasionally.

Chilean Rose Tarantula

The Chilean rose tarantula has lots of red hairs all over its body and legs. It is also known as the rose hair tarantula.

Where in the World?

The Chilean rose tarantula lives in the desert and scrublands of northern Chile and neighboring regions in South America.

The Chilean rose has urticating hairs, but it is unlikely to flick them because it is a docile spider.

24

Breed Profile

The Chilean rose is calm and docile. It moves slowly and is a good tarantula for beginners to keep as a pet. It is a ground-dwelling spider with a leg span of about 5 inches (13 cm). Females live for around 20 to 25 years, and males for only around five.

Looking After Me

The tank needs to be kept at about 75 to 80°F (24 to 27°C). It can be cooler at night.

- ☑ Humidity in the tank is best around 65 to 75 percent.

- ☑ The Chilean rose eats crickets, mealworms, and other large insects such as cockroaches.

Mexican Redknee Tarantula

This colorful tarantula is named for the red bands around its legs. It looks like it has red knees!

Where in the World?

The Mexican redknee tarantula comes from the Pacific coast of Mexico. It lives in drier regions where there is little vegetation.

The Mexican redknee tarantula is often used in movies as a spider to scare people!

26

Breed Profile

The Mexican redknee is a ground-dwelling tarantula. It is usually docile and calm, but it will flick urticating hairs if it feels stressed. It has a leg span of 5 to 5.5 inches (13 to 14 cm). Females can live for between 15 and 25 years. Males live for up to 10 years.

Looking After Me

Keep the temperature in the tank around 75 to 80°F (24 to 27°C). It can be cooler at night.

- ✓ The humidity in the tank is best at around 65 to 75 percent.

- ✓ Adult spiders will eat crickets and other large insects, as well as the occasional pinky mouse.

Make It!
Bug Hotel

Build an amazing bug hotel from materials
you can find outside or in the hardware store.
The insects and spiders in your yard will love it!

You Will Need:

Old bricks or large, flat stones
Planks of wood
Straw
Twigs
Pine cones
Moss
Dry leaves
Tree bark
Bamboo sticks

1 Choose a shady place for your bug hotel next to a wall or fence.

2 Put some bricks on the ground. Place a plank across the top.

3 Add more bricks and planks until you have three or more levels. Each level can have different materials on it.

4 Tie bunches of twigs together or put them in cardboard tubes. Put these on one or two levels.

5 Make a nest of dry leaves, moss, and tree bark on another level.

6 Put pine cones and straw on another level. Add small tubes such as reeds or bamboo sticks for bees to use.

Your bug hotel should fill up with visitors over the weeks. Check it every few days, but try not to disturb the guests.

Bricks

Planks

Did You Know?

Insects have been on Earth for about 350 million years. They are the most successful and numerous animals on the planet. Some studies say there may be 200 million insects for every person alive today!

The golden orb-web spider spins webs from 3 to 6.5 feet (1 to 2 m) wide. This spider is thought to make the strongest silk.

Scientists have named about 1.5 million different species of insects. There are many more they haven't yet discovered—there may be as many as 30 million kinds of insects!

Insects have three body parts and six legs. Spiders have two body parts and eight legs.

The earliest fossil cockroach to have been found is about 280 million years old. That's about 80 million years older than the first dinosaurs!

There are about 39,500 different species of spiders on Earth.

Most spiders live alone, but some work together to build huge webs. Thousands of spiders work on the web and share the prey that is caught in it.

Some insects, such as water striders, are able to walk on water! The water strider has tiny hairs on its legs. The hairs trap air bubbles, allowing the insect to float!

The praying mantis is the only insect that can turn its head.

Glossary

abdomen largest part of a spider's body, to which the legs are attached.

antenna (pl: antennae) thin, sensitive body part on the head of an insect, used for feeling or smelling.

aphid small insect that feeds on plants.

docile not aggressive.

fragile easily hurt or damaged.

hardy strong, not easily hurt.

humidity the amount of moisture in the air.

insecticide a substance used to kill harmful insects.

leg span for spiders, the distance from the tip of one leg to the tip of the leg on the opposite side.

mealworm young form of a beetle, often used as pet food.

molt lose a covering of skin or hair to make way for new growth.

moss small flowerless green plant.

peat brown material made from decaying plants.

pinky mouse young mouse without fur.

scrubland area with small bushes and trees.

silk (of spider) strong fiber produced by spiders to build webs.

species group of animals or plants that are similar and are able to produce young.

substrate layer of material that lines the bottom of a tank.

terrarium enclosure for keeping small land animals.

tropical occurring in or relating to the tropics— warm areas of the world close to the equator.

urticating causing stinging or itching.

Further Resources

Books

Calver, Paul.
Insects and Spiders
(Visual Explorers). Barron's
Educational Series, 2016.

**Lomberg, Michelle and
Katie Gillespie.**
Spider (Caring for My Pet).
AV2 by Weigl, 2016.

Parker, Steve.
Insects and Spiders
(100 Facts You Should Know).
Gareth Stevens Publishing, 2015.

Websites

Due to the changing nature of Internet links,
PowerKids Press has developed an online list
of websites related to the subject of this
book. This site is updated regularly.
Please use this link to access the list:

www.powerkidslinks.com/cpfk/insects

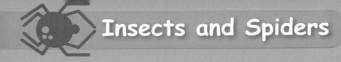

Index

A B
Africa 20
Antarctica 14
Arctic 14
bedding 9

C
Central America 22
Central American Giant
  cave cockroach 15
Chile 24
Chilean rose tarantula
  24–25
cockroaches 4, 6, 7, 8, 11,
  13, 15, 20–21, 29
Costa Rica 22

D
deserts 14, 15
dinosaurs 29
dried food 11, 21

F G
feeding 10–11
food 11, 21
forests 15, 16
fossil 29
fruit 11, 21
Goliath tarantula 14
grasslands 15

H
health 12–13
heat mats 7

Honduran curly hair
  tarantula 22–23
Honduras 22
housing 6, 8–9
humidity 7, 9, 13, 19, 23,
  25, 27

I
Indian walking stick 4
Indonesia 18
insecticide 10
insects 4, 5, 29

L M
leaf insects 4, 6, 8, 10, 14
live food 7, 10
Madagascar 20
Madagascar hissing
  cockroach 20–21
Malaysia 18
mantids 7, 9, 10, 12, 15
Mexican redknee
  tarantula 4, 26–27
Mexico 26
molting 8, 12, 13

O P
orchid mantis 15, 18–19
polar regions 14
praying mantid 18–19, 29

R S
rain forests 18, 22
rose hair tarantula 24

sickness 12
South America 14, 24
Southeast Asia 14, 16, 18
spiders 4, 5, 9, 11, 29
stick insects 4, 6, 8, 10,
  12, 15, 16–17
substrate 8

T U
tarantulas 4, 5, 6, 7, 11,
  13, 14, 22–23, 24–25,
  26–27
temperature 7, 9, 17, 19,
  21, 23, 25, 27
thermometer 7
tropical regions 14
urticating hairs 23, 24, 27

V
vegetables 11, 21
Vietnam 16
Vietnamese walking stick
  16–17

W
water 10, 11, 21
water striders 29
webs 29
wooly tarantula 22